Dinosongs

Poems to Celebrate

A T. REX NAMED SUE™

The Field Museum

STONE HOUSE
PRODUCTIONS, LLC

SCHOLASTIC

For Clava
— K.M.C.

To Marcie and the kids
— K.V.

With special thanks to
Cheryl Carlesimo, Bernette Ford, Amy Louis,
Craig Rogers, Sharon Sullivan, and Felisia Wesson.

Library of Congress Cataloging-in-Publication Data available
ISBN 0-439-19264-1

10 9 8 7 6 5 4 3 2 1   00 01 02 03 04

Printed in China
First printing, August 2000

SCHOLASTIC INC. AND THE FIELD MUSEUM PRESENT

Dinosongs

Poems to Celebrate
A T. REX NAMED SUE™

BY **K.M. CROTTY** • **ILLUSTRATED** BY **KURT VARGO**

SCHOLASTIC INC.
New York Toronto London Auckland Sydney
Mexico City New Delhi Hong Kong

BIRTH OF SUE

The silent egg inside the nest
Stirs the human child's breast.
It harbors neither fowl nor fish,
But every child's secret wish.

Tyrannosaurus, you delight
The young with your ferocious might.
Your dreadful jaws and mammoth size
Astonish them and tantalize....

The little tyrant rex awaits
The sparkling lights of Earth and sky.
The dino-hatchling contemplates
The jungle she will terrify.

And in this Mesozoic zoo,
The grunts and bellows make her wince:
Blasts of the paleo-hullabaloo—
A symphony like nothing since!

YOUTH
SUE EXPLORES HER WORLD

From a green meadow, Sue set out
To see what life was all about.
The Late Cretaceous skies were blue
Where gliding pterodactyls flew.

Beyond the waving ferns, she sees
Alamosaurus snack on trees.
And packs of pachycephalosaurs
Frolic near Montana's shores.

One day, when she has mammoth jaws,
She'll rule the roost by jungle laws.
But now the toddler T. rex tries
To swat at darting dragonflies.
Believe me, all the world respects
You now, Tyrannosaurus rex!

COMPETITION FOR FOOD

The Troodon's intelligence
Provides this dino's best defense.
Its agile mind and sharpened claws
Give even mighty monsters pause....

While T. rex sates her appetite,
On fallen prey with blood-stained bite,
The Troodon, with watchful eye,
Attempts to filch a piece of thigh.

Sue roars and bares her eight-inch teeth,
To terrorize the dino-thief.
But Troodon, retreating quick,
Usurps the carcass in its grip.

Troodon, your wits perplex
A most Tyranno-sorry rex!

PARASAUROLOPHUS CHASE

The Parasaurolophus' big, bony crest
Makes dinosaur music when air is expressed.
These talkative duckbills converse with their kind
In deep bassoon rumblings whenever inclined.
Their music exerts the most varied appeal,
And Sue, the Tyrannosaur, thinks: "It's a meal!"

Look! The omnivorous, dreadful carnivorous
Tyrann-horribilis chases her prey.
And Parasaurolophus (really, like all of us)
Gallops in hopes of outliving the day —
This thirty-foot wonder now thunders away!

And *if* he escapes, he later reflects,
He'll give a wide berth to Tyrannosaur rex.

BATTLE WITH THE TRICERATOPS

What thunderous grunting resounds on the plains?
It's dull and it deafens. It waxes and wanes.
A horde of Triceratops sever and gnash,
Devouring magnolias, laurel, and ash.
This herbivore's armored: Its head's overgrown
With three sharpened spikes and a ruffle of bone.
The mightiest monsters it fiercely deflects,
And even assaults by Tyrannosaur rex....

As T. rex advances, preparing to kill,
Triceratops bristles her terrible frill,
And swipes with her horns at the enemy's chest,
And rips the aggressor, and pierces her breast.
Sue bellows in pain, and attacks in a rage—
Yes, dinner was war in the dinosaur age.

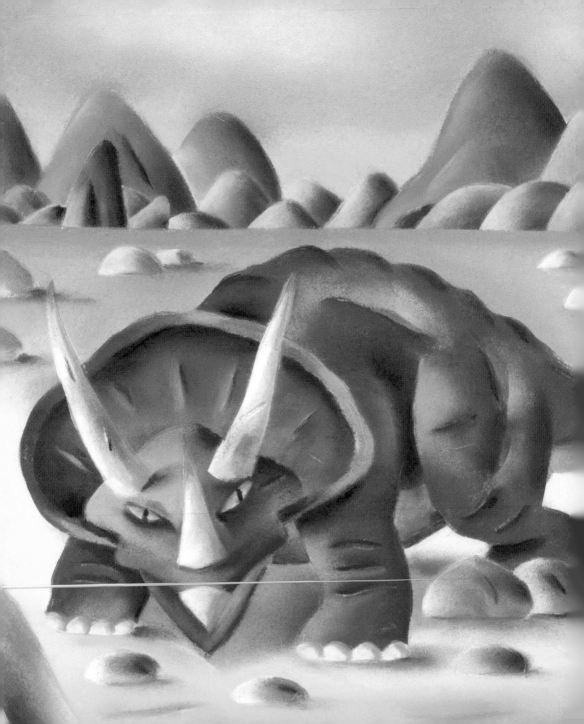

TWILIGHT
OF THE DINOSAURS

The iron law that none shall last
Consigns Cretaceous to the past.
It saps the strength of fighting brutes,
And rocks the planet to its roots.
The ancient beast with bleary eyes
Sees ruin falling from the skies....

Tyrant lizard, sovereign beast,
Now your savage life has ceased.
Violence, appetite, and rage
Are stilled by time and quenched by age.
Limbs that dealt a thousand blows
Are folded in an odd repose....

Soon, the world that made your might
Will chill its air and dim its light—
The species dies and nevermore
Will Earth resound with Rex's roar.

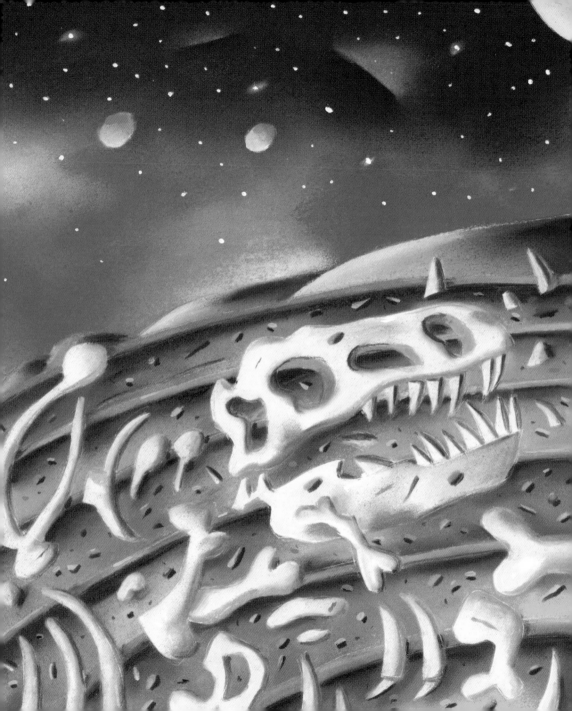

Dawn of a New World

A billion dawns have lit the skies
And life, resurgent, multiplies.
The mammals, once a timid race,
When dinosaurs held pride of place,
Have risen from their humble birth,
To take possession of the Earth—

The ape, the tiger, horse, and hind,
And, in the future, humankind,
Whose energies and intellects
Will conjure up Tyranno rex.
Their wise will coax the silent bone
To speak what none has ever known.
And Rex, recalled, will move among
The dream-lives of the old and young.

A T. REX NAMED SUE AND THE DINOSONGS

Our story took place long, long ago — in fact, about 67 million years ago. How much of it is true? Well, Dinosaur SUE, the heroine, really existed: You can see her awesome skeleton at The Field Museum of Chicago. All of the other characters in these poems, too, were animals that SUE might really have met. Each of them existed in the Late Cretaceous period and lived in the western United States, the same part of the world as SUE.

When the toddler SUE set out for a walk, there were indeed dragonflies to swat. SUE's neighbors (and, no doubt, sometimes her dinners) included the Troodon, the Triceratops, and the Parasaurolophus. As her skeleton shows, SUE probably lived to an old age — she's the "ancient beast with bleary eye" in the sixth poem. And she was one of the last of the dinosaurs. Not long after her death, dinosaurs disappeared from the face of the earth.

So, while these *Dinosongs* are a work of the imagination, they stay close to the known facts, with the help of The Field Museum of Chicago. These poems were originally written to accompany a piece of music composed to celebrate SUE's arrival at The Field Museum. Unveiled to the public in May of 2000, SUE stands tall once again — a breathtaking testament to a long ago time when these powerful creatures ruled the earth.